Forgiveness is the Key to Freedom

How to release yourself from
a self-inflicted prison.

Shenita Atherton

Forgiveness is the Key to Freedom

Copyright © 2022 Shenita Atherton.

All rights reserved. No portion of this book may be reproduced, stored in a retrieval system, or transmitted in any form or by any means—electronic, mechanical, photocopy, recording, scanning, or other—except for brief quotations in critical reviews or articles, or as specifically allowed by the U. S. Copyright Act of 1976, as amended, without the prior written permission of the publisher. Scripture quotations are taken from the King James version of the Bible.

Ordering Information:
For details, contact *shenita@shenitaatherton.com*

Interior and Cover Design: Alberto Bastasa
Editor: Tiffany Starks

ISBN Paperback: 979-8-42799-821-5

Printed in the United States of America.

First Edition

Contents

Acknowledgements v
Foreword vii
Introduction ix

Chapter 1: Acknowledge That There
 is a Problem 1
Chapter 2: Acknowledge Your
 Contribution to the Problem 13
Chapter 3: How to Forgive Yourself 22
Chapter 4: Forgiveness Will Set You Free! 30
Chapter 5: Learn to Identify God's
 Hand in the Midst of Chaos 41
Chapter 6: Forgiveness Does Not
 Always Equate to Reconnection 46

Prayers for Forgiveness 51
Closure 54
30 Keys to Freedom 56

Acknowledgements

This book is one that the Lord impressed upon my heart to write and share with the world as a resource to help individuals demolish the root of unforgiveness in their lives and provide practical tools, tips, and advice that will lead them on their journey to forgiveness. I would not have been able to write this book without the unwavering support of my beloved husband, Dr. Marlon Atherton, and our amazing children, Marlon Jr., Sarai, and Malik. Thank you for allowing me the time and space with plenty of grace to complete this assignment. I would like to thank and acknowledge my dear friend, Daphne H., who also encouraged me to write this book. After sharing my life experiences with her, she said I had no choice but to write this book. She believes it will be a tremendous help to others and will help encourage others to realize there is beauty at the end of the pain they may be experiencing. Lastly, to my dear friend and sister from another mother, Dr. Annie F., who was always there during this journey to lend a listening ear and offer unending love and support along the way, I cannot say thank you enough. May God continue to bless you all exceedingly and abundantly with more than you could ever ask or think!

Foreword

Dr. Shenita Atherton is a remarkable woman of God. She is a gifted and anointed teacher, mentor, leader, and friend! Her wisdom and depth of knowledge are profound. Her desire to teach others the Word of God is evident, and she has a wonderful way of presenting the Word in a way that brings understanding and application. I am thankful for the person she is and what she has meant to me over the years. Her book, Forgiveness is the Key to Freedom, is one that I highly recommend.

Shenita shares her personal experience of being a victim of unforgiveness and how she was able to forgive and break free from that cycle. The book provides exercises and tools for readers to learn how to forgive others and themselves so that they can live a life of freedom.

The book starts with the premise that in order to be set free, we must first forgive. It then goes on to explain what it means to forgive and how we are unable to move forward in our lives if we are not willing to do so. It does a great job of explaining the process of forgiveness.

Forgiveness is the key to a happy and fulfilling life. It is the greatest gift you can give to yourself and to others. When we forgive, we are releasing resentment, hurt, and anger. I'm so glad that I read the book! Forgiveness is the Key to Freedom is an amazing book that has helped me to understand and practice forgiveness in my own life. Shenita gives us many ways to begin the process of forgiving ourselves, our spouses, parents, siblings, children, and friends.

The author's personal anecdotes and easy-to-understand analogies make this book enjoyable and relatable. Written with a light and inspirational tone, this book is easy to read and an enjoyable journey into the world of forgiveness. If you are holding on to past hurtful incidents by individuals you trusted and loved, then I recommend that you read this book. Forgiveness is not for the other person; it is for us!

Dr. Marlon Atherton
President | CORE Kingdom University

Introduction

Forgiveness. Yeah, that infamous "F" word that makes some cringe at its very sound. Forgiveness is defined as the action or process of forgiving or being forgiven. The Bible tells us in Matthew 18:21-22 that we are to forgive our neighbor seventy times seven, which ultimately means we should be forgiving our neighbor, family member, friend, etc. 490 times in one day.

> *Then came Peter to him, and said, Lord, how oft shall my brother sin against me, and I forgive him? till seven times? Jesus saith unto him, I say not unto thee, Until seven times: but, Until seventy times seven. Matthew 18:21-22 KJV*

Whew, how many times Lord? You might be asking yourself how can someone offend someone that many times in one day? Well, my friend, you would be very surprised. Forgiving others and yourself for that matter can sometimes be a very challenging task. The weight of everything that may have taken place can cause you to hold onto all the baggage of the past instead of letting it go. It is a process that you must be willing to take if you would like God to forgive you of the things you did to break His heart.

> *For if you forgive others their trespasses [their reckless and willful sins], your heavenly Father will also forgive you. Matthew 6:14 AMP*

God's Word is very clear on how to handle forgiveness with specific details on how often we should extend forgiveness to others, no matter what atrocities and wars they have waged against you, no matter what they may have said, or what hurtful things they may have done. I know that can seem like a huge pill to swallow, but obedience will open doors in your life and set you up for success. Sometimes you must obey your way out of situations and trust that God will see you through.

> *And Samuel said, Hath the LORD as great delight in burnt offerings and sacrifices, as in obey-*

ing the voice of the LORD? Behold, to obey is better than sacrifice, and to hearken than the fat of rams. 1 Samuel 15:22

The intent of this book is to equip you with the tools, strategies, and knowledge you need to live a life of freedom. In this book, I will share some mistakes I have made in this area and explain how God opened my eyes and gave me a new perspective on this matter. You will learn how to live a life extending forgiveness as soon as an offense is identified. Some people fear forgiveness and push it completely aside because they believe forgiveness equates to an open door with a ticket to a front row seat back into their lives, and it does not. Forgiveness means that you decided to be obedient to God no matter how hard a task that may be, love others as He has instructed you to love, and live in freedom.

An unforgiving heart has become a huge stumbling block in the lives of so many because they struggle with the how and why of it all. As a matter of fact, unforgiveness is a very dangerous thing. When you allow an offense to fester and grow, you have just given satan the permission he needed to take precedence in your life and help you wage a full-fledged war against yourself. Sometimes, we can become so fixated on a problem that we forget that there is a man than can rectify the direst situations and turn them around for our good. Some struggle with an internal battle every day of whether they are even worthy of forgiveness because of the things that have taken place in their lives. Others may struggle with learning how to forgive someone because, in their mind, they have been hurt beyond what can be repaired, so they hold unforgiveness over the head of others as a pawn. I have also found myself in the same scenario several times in my life. Walk with me on this journey as I share my own story of how I overcame this very thing and learned how to forgive even when some people in my life hurt me to my core and never fully accepted the reality of the damage that was caused and have not apologized. Oh, this is going to be a journey for sure. Come along for the ride as I show you how you can be victorious and how you will win in the end.

Forgiveness is something I wrestled with for a very long time because as soon as I would get to a place of peace and calm, it felt like I was slapped with a tsunami of unfortunate events, the reset button was hit, and there I was amid the same old nasty cycle yet again. What I learned is that forgiveness will set you free in every area of your life – mind, body, and soul. Holding on to scenarios and situations that you have endured in the past and keeping them on constant replay in your mind is like planting a bomb in your home and waiting for your neighbor's home to explode. While you are concocting plans for how the explosion should take place, your neighbor is living comfortably, enjoying life to the fullest without a care in the world. The enemy will trick you into believing it is okay to wreak havoc on their lives and recruit others to do the same, all because you do not have peace in your heart and mind about what has caused you to become bitter and angry. You may spend countless days and precious moments holding on to things of the past, which has done nothing but keep you busy running yourself ragged day in and day out thinking about how you will get revenge or make them feel the pain you have felt. Can I let you in on a little secret? It, whatever that "it" may be, is not worth your peace. Get your peace back. Love and bless those who have hurt you even if your love for them is displayed from afar.

> *But I say unto you, Love your enemies, bless them that curse you, do good to them that hate you, and pray for them which despitefully use you, and persecute you;*
> *Matthew 5:44*

My heart's desire is that this book will bring peace, healing, and deliverance to your hearts, minds, homes, family units, relationships, marriages, and ultimately every area of your lives. I decree and declare that peace and healing is your portion, the chains that have held you hostage for so long are broken now in the name of Jesus. May you be equipped with tools, skills, and divine strategies to help you overcome the tricks, plans, and schemes of the enemy. Psalm 91 says that God will protect us from the snares of the fowler, the one that comes to cause us harm. Remember, you are more than a conqueror through Christ Jesus, and you can do all things if you continue to lean on the Lord because He alone will give you the strength to do those things that appear to be too difficult to handle. What the enemy means for evil, God will always turn around for your good.

> *But as for you, ye thought evil against me; but God meant it unto good, to bring to pass, as it is*

this day, to save much people alive.
Genesis 50:20

Trust Him and allow Him to surprise you. There is no crime you have ever committed or unjust you have caused that will keep you away from the love of the Father. If you keep Him at the very center of your life, always placing Him first in all that you do, He will restore your soul. There is nothing anyone can say or do to change what God says about you or decide how He chooses to bless you because they look at your past and deem you unworthy. You are needed, you matter, God has great plans for you, and He will see you through in Jesus' name. Amen!

Chapter 1

Acknowledge That There is a Problem

Curiosity sparked my mind about the word "acknowledgment". I wanted to know exactly what it entailed, so I looked it up and here is what I found. Acknowledgment means the acceptance of truth or existence of something. Until you can accept the truth or existence of a matter, you will remain stuck in a pattern and cycle until no end. Why is acknowledgment so hard? A safe assumption might be that no one likes to admit they were wrong, which is a very dangerous thing. This is connected to pride, which we will talk about later in the book.

> *"If a fellow believer hurts you, go and tell him—work it out between the two of you. If he lis-*

tens, you've made a friend. If he won't listen, take one or two others along so that the presence of witnesses will keep things honest, and try again. If he still won't listen, tell the church. If he won't listen to the church, you'll have to start over from scratch, confront him with the need for repentance, and offer again God's forgiving love. Matthew 18:15-17 MSG

The scriptures give us some foundational instructions on how to address conflict in our lives. Matthew 18:15-17 says: "If another believer sins against you, go privately and point out the offense. If the other person listens and confesses it, you have won that person back. But if you are unsuccessful, take one or two others with you and go back again, so that everything you say may be confirmed by two or three witnesses. If the person still refuses to listen, take your case to the church. Then if he or she will not accept the church's decision, treat that person as a pagan or a corrupt tax collector." You don't want to skip these crucial steps that you must take to make amends no matter how challenging it may seem.

The problem you may run into is that some people do not want to address issues head on and get to the root of the problem. Instead of going through the proper channels, information is disseminated through the wrong channels, and you end up with a bigger problem than you started with (ask me how I know). You must slash the problem from the root to get down to the truth of the matter before offense sets in. Jesus gives us a great foundation and guidelines for dealing with those who have hurt and abused us. These guidelines were not established to send us all on a rampage attacking everyone that has hurt us in any way, but they were established to ultimately get us back into right fellowship with one another so that we can live in harmony. We should all be open and welcome constructive criticism with open arms even when we are the one behind the hurt that has been caused in the lives of those around us. What I had to realize was that my truth and peace strategies were not the same for everyone else in my life. I had to meet individuals where they were because everyone did not have the same revelation that I did. This was a learning process for me, and l must tell you this was no easy task, to say the least. No matter how challenging a situation may appear, I have learned that the first step to overcoming hard situations is being willing to acknowledge that there is a problem. Yes, the first step to deliverance is acknowledgement, because to be set free and delivered from any situation you are challenged with, you must first be willing to admit and acknowledge that there is a problem. Avoidance of certain situations and conversations because of fear of conflict will not make a situation any better. In fact, it can make it even worse, like that crack on your windshield from that rock that you have ignored for months because it appeared contained on the surface. Over time, that crack begins to spread and ultimately destroys the entire windshield. If addressed early on, it could have been repaired at a much lower cost, but now you have a hefty price to pay. I have also learned that most physical battles we face in life start in the mind first. I once heard someone say, "Thoughts become words, words turn into actions." Over time, those thoughts, words, and actions can become weapons we use to cause destruction, which is all a part of satan's master plan. My motto and mantra for life is "Speak Life," yet I was in this place where I found it quite challenging to speak life in such dire circumstances. Although I knew that life and death are in the power of the tongue and that I had the power to control certain situations by believing in my heart that God had the power to remove those mountains in my life, I was stuck. There is a reason why God referenced the sycamore tree in Luke 17:6.

And the Lord said, "If ye had faith as a grain of mustard seed, ye might say unto this sycamine tree, be thou plucked up by the root, and be thou planted in the sea; and it should obey you." Luke 17:6

The roots of a sycamine tree are so deeply rooted that it is almost impossible to pluck them up. The roots run so deep that it is best to plant this type of tree as far away from buildings as possible. That is what happens to us sometimes regarding forgiveness. Just like the roots of the sycamine tree, we have planted roots so deep in our hearts that sometimes it seems impossible to pluck out the bitterness and hardening of heart that has taken place as a result of pain. If you have faith the size of that small mustard seed, you will be able to speak to that mountain of unforgiveness in your lives, command it to be removed, and it has no choice but to be removed. Remember, what may seem impossible for you is not impossible with God! Let's go back for a moment. While I was experiencing relationship challenges with some family members, I became very discouraged because I felt like no one was willing to admit their contributions to problems that we were experiencing. There was more finger pointing, behind the scenes chatter, and false accusations floating around than acknowledgement of what was taking place. I thought there was a quick fix to the problems we were experiencing, but what I soon discovered was those years upon years of dysfunctional relationship dynamics kept us all in perpetual toxic cycles because of lack of acknowledgement. I should have been trusting and believing that God would do what He said He would do and continued to actively speak His word over those challenges and called those things that be not as though they were. I hit a dead end and it felt like I was stuck between a rock and a hard place, but I can tell you that through it all, ***forgiveness was the key to freedom,*** although I had not discovered it yet!

I had been going in perpetual cycles of toxicity, pain, rejection, hurt, deception, strife, lies, and false accusations, and I wanted out! Satan had me right where he wanted me, nestled tightly in his venomous grip of deception. Have you ever heard the phrase "hurt people hurt people"? Well, that is exactly what I did. Every time someone who I assumed had my best interest at heart hurt me through that recipe I call "disaster," I would clap right back and get them where I knew it would hurt. I would use my mouth as a weapon of mass destruction. One day I cried out to God because I had gotten to a place of pure desperation. You see, this was not new to me; it had become so familiar that I became numb to a certain extent waiting for the next episode of chaos.

One day, I had gotten to a place of despair. My heart was screaming and crying out for answers. I had shared my feelings with some, took jabs from others with accusations and finger pointing, and I even questioned God and asked Him several times: "Are you watching?? Do you see this? Do you hear what is being said?" Yep, I asked God if He was watching as if He does not know all and see all. What was I thinking? Conversations with some friends and loved ones did nothing but keep me in this vicious cycle like a hamster in a cage spinning on a wheel and going nowhere fast. I was furious, but this battle was not my own. If I wanted change, if I wanted God to handle it, I had to take my hands off, which was easier said than done. I held on to this rucksack of dysfunction for much longer than I should have. As a matter of fact, I should have never picked it up and carried it around in the first place; it was time to let it go. Little did I know that what I was doing was placing myself in a prison cell waiting for others to be punished. What I later learned was that we should never have an internal timer waiting for the clock to run out on those who have hurt us so they can be punished. Let's look at Job. He experienced much hardship in his life at a certain period when things were going seemingly well for him and when he was very prosperous. His friends started out encouraging him, but then they all began to falsely accuse him and were confident in telling him that he had to have done something wrong for God to issue such hard judgment against him. How Job handled the situation after listening to their false claims is so profound. Instead of cursing his friends and developing bitterness in his heart and an ill-will towards them, he prayed for them. It was after that life altering moment of prayer that God released Job from his captivity and blessed him with twice as much as he had before (Job 42:10).

I had to keep reminding myself that no matter how bad things looked, God still had my back and He was going to see me through, but I had to do my part. I began praying for my enemies and those who offended me. I began to wish God's absolute best for them no matter what they had said or done to me. I then realized that God could handle the situation much better than I ever could.

Oftentimes, we try to fix situations through our own power and might. What I discovered the hard way was that we cannot change people. The only one we need to focus on changing is ourselves and that was a big pill to swallow. I learned to keep this prayer hidden in my heart although I found myself struggling sometimes: "God grant me the serenity to accept the things I cannot change, the courage to change the things I can, and the wisdom to know the difference." I would literally stop myself in my own tracks and say, "Girl, stop. Shenita, be quiet," because somewhere deep down inside, I wanted answers. The biggest question I had was WHY? I would run myself weary with the whys and why nots. I wanted an apology, thinking it would soothe my soul, but I never got it. The best thing we can do when we feel we have been mistreated, neglected, misunderstood, rejected, or abused, etc. is to let God fight the battle for us and let Him carry the weight of despair and open our hearts so we can forgive. I can honestly say this is much easier said than done, yet I had to be confident knowing that I could do all things through Christ who would give me the strength to do just that.

I can do all things through Christ which strengthens me.
Philippians 4:13

Once you can acknowledge that there is a problem, whether you caused it or not, you are on the right path. Acknowledgement can help get you out of the bondage you are entangled in and lead you into a place of peace and freedom. Often, we become so fixated on the other person. We want them to acknowledge the wrong they did to us, but God is trying to get us to see that no matter what they did, we must forgive them in order to be set free. Taking this first step is crucial at this point in the battle. It will cause less heartache and pain and prevent you from missing out on what God has for you. There are so many golden nuggets nestled in the Word of God, but if you do not plug in and get connected, you may miss the keys and strategies you need in times like these.

> *Pride goes before destruction,*
> *and a haughty spirit before a fall.*
> *Proverbs 16:18*

Pride is the very thing that keeps most from acknowledging that there is problem. The spirit of pride will cause you to focus on everything they did wrong and will have you lifting yourself up higher than others, thinking you are perfect, and thinking that something is wrong with everyone except you. Pride is a very nasty spirit. Your view can become so clouded that in your eyes, you have done no wrong and the other person is the one who needs to get themselves together. Some people do not want it to be known that they have done the things they have done, so denial becomes easier than acknowledgment, but that is not the place you want to be in. If you are not will willing to acknowledge that there is a problem and identify your contribution to the matter, there is little room for growth and development.

I was very curious about the word "pride", so I looked up the Greek definition, and the meaning of pride is superiority and arrogance. Pride will cause you to lose those valuable people in your life and cause you break divine covenants and divine connections and lose all that you deem important. The Bible says that pride is the very thing that will cause people to fall. I encourage you to do a self-assessment of your life and ask God if there are any areas of pride that you need to get rid of. The moment you surrender your will for God's will, your life will change for the better.

Here are some tips to help you acknowledge the problem and identify healthy solutions.

....

1. Handle misunderstandings with others sooner rather than later. Take a trusted individual with you who you believe has your best interest at heart but is not afraid to tell you the truth.
2. Identify the problem. Find out where things went wrong.
3. Have an open heart and mind to receive what others have to say.
4. Ask for forgiveness and extend forgiveness to others.

Chapter 2

Acknowledge Your Contribution to the Problem

To acknowledge your contribution to the problem, you must first have a clear understanding of the word "contribution." The word "contribution" means the part played by a person or thing in bringing about a result or helping something to advance. This will lead you to ask yourself a few questions about your role and involvement in the matter. Freedom is predicated on your willingness to be set free. You cannot release a bound person unless they can first acknowledge that they want to be set free.

Do you remember the story about the Israelites? I believe they were the poster children for a lesson learned the hard way. Disobedience, grumbles, and complaints gripped them at their very core, and they found themselves right in the middle of torment and a self-inflicted battle – all because they chose to be stubborn. They got in their own way and traveled 40 years in the wilderness on what was really an 11-day journey. I don't know about you, but I don't want to extend any journey I take like that. We're talking about 40 years, not 40 days or 40 minutes. Geesh! After about six hours on the road, I am ready to call it a day, so I will kindly pass on 40 years. This was exactly what I was doing to myself though. I was right in the middle of a self-inflicted battle because of what was going on around me and I couldn't see the break of dawn; it was nowhere near the horizon. I had to realize that I was traveling on a journey like the Israelites, taking much longer to get to my destination of forgiveness because, in my eyes, it was just too tedious a task to forgive those who had yet to apologize for things they did to cause hurt and pain. You see, I was hurt to my core, and I often found myself wanting those who hurt me and my family to feel the hurt we felt. I also wanted acknowledgment, clarification, and explanations – some of which I never received. I led myself to believe that I deserved these things. Feelings of entitlement rose within me, and I felt like that was the least that could be done at that time. Who knew I would have to learn that there will be times in life when you'll have to forgive people for things they did that they never had the heart to sincerely acknowledge and apologize for. One of the worst things you can do when apologizing to anyone is saying, "If I have done anything to hurt you, I apologize," especially if you know that you have wronged them. Apologizing this way is rooted in pride. If you are unsure if your words or actions caused someone to be offended, the best thing you can do is have a conversation with them and ask them, get clarity, and then sincerely apologize for hurting them and vice versa.

Unending questions ran around in circles in my mind during that season in my life. Why can't they just address it? Why can't we just talk about it? Why are they behaving this way? Why, why, why? While praying and seeking God on the matter, those words were on replay in my mind. What I learned along the way was that it was not about "them" anymore – it never was. I had given "them" too much power. I had allowed "them" to infiltrate my heart, my mind, my soul, and my very being, and it was time to let it go. It was never about "them" anyway and was always about me from the very start. Why did I let "them" have a key to my heart and let "them" come in and cause me to act contrary to what I knew was right? The hard truth was that I had to take a hard look at "me". I was about to get "me" in trouble with God by worrying and wondering about what everyone was or was not doing. One very important piece to this gigantic puzzle was my contribution to the matter.

As I pondered this, many questions arose. What had I done or said that could have added to the problem? How had I used my mouth as a weapon of mass destruction and cursed others when I should have blessed them? What had I failed to do that contributed to the chaos? What senseless acts did I commit out of frustration that could have been the very thing that caused someone else to fall in this boat of despair with me? I had to ask myself some hard questions because all along I was so fixated on "them", as if I had done no wrong. I was very reactive in my stance. If I would find out that something was said, a lie was told, or something was done negatively towards me and my family, I would retaliate with my words. I would retaliate with my actions. I would retaliate because I kept telling myself that there was absolutely no way I was going to take this mistreatment any longer. As I look back over everything, there were plenty of things I could have done differently like not being bothered by it all in the first place and never allowing it an opportunity to disrupt my peace.

As a result of all the things I experienced in my life up to that point, I was at my wits end and I had enough. I often questioned God and asked why I was always the target because that is how I truly felt. I asked why everyone was so fixated on what I was doing, who I was talking to, and where I was going, etc. Why could I not just live my life without the condemnation, judgment, ridicule, lies, and false accusations, and without being put on the chopping block for others to chop away at me and ridicule me with their actions and their negative words? The funny part about it is why I ever thought I was exempt from all this in the first place. The Word of God tells us that Christ was beaten, bruised, spat on, and crucified just for us. He endured pain and torment and was crucified for sins He did not commit. If Christ endured such hardship, it is only a matter of time before us believers face adversity as well. It is not a matter of if, but when, because it is inevitable. This toxic cycle led me into periods of isolation time and time again. I would purposely ignore all forms of communication just to maintain a certain level of peace and stability in my life. I needed peace, and peace for me sometimes meant dodging that phone call and not responding to that text until I was good and ready spiritually and mentally.

    I learned many valuable lessons in that season. At times when I just needed to talk about what I was dealing with, I would use bad judgment and reach out to the wrong person who did not fully understand confidentiality. Before I knew it, there I was again entangled and caught up in this recipe for disaster all because I shared my heart to the wrong person. At times, I was convinced that I was sharing my heart in confidence, but little by little I learned the hard way that I was not, and if I am being honest here, many of those conversations were spent gossiping. Yes, let me be the first to tell the truth. Because I was hurt, I began venting to who I perceived as trusted individuals and they helped keep me in the toxic cycle I was already in. They helped me talk badly about certain individuals. I found myself constantly in what seemed like a never-ending battle because I used poor judgment and was not in tune with God. I let my feelings and emotions take precedence in my life, which was a very poor decision on my part. During this time, I was upset and started playing the blame game all over again until I realized it was my fault for opening my mouth and sharing those things in the first place. Reality hit me hard yet again. Instead of blaming others, I had to realize that I was the one at fault because I had failed to truly turn my burdens over to God, trusting that He would see me through. I had to take another hard look at ***me*** and not "them" yet again. It had been a journey full of ups, downs, joy, sadness, triumph, and gloom, and through it all there were still many lessons to be learned. Just as a baby is learning to walk, first they get their balance and then they gain enough confidence to stand up on their own. Then, before you know, they have gained enough courage to take that first step. Sometimes that first step is met with a hard and unexpected fall, but guess what? That baby does not give up. They may cry for a little while and they may be disappointed, but they get up and attempt to take that next step again. Talk about determination. You see, there is a lesson to be learned in every situation and circumstance you face in life and the question we must ask ourselves is, "Did you get it?" Did you really grasp the blessing and the lesson that was intended to carry you through the next season in your life? Or did you just bypass the lesson altogether because your mind was too clouded and you were too tired to put forth enough effort to care? Did it even matter to you at all? Or were you just complacent and numb and did not give two hoots about anyone or anything in that present moment? We must ask ourselves these hard questions sometimes if we ever want to make it to the other side of whatever we are facing in life. One day during my quiet time, the Holy Spirit whispered in my ear, "Vengeance is mine says the Lord." It was in that moment that I let it all go after years and years of residue. I truly *FORGAVE* them all! It was at that moment where I felt like a huge burden was lifted and I felt a sigh of relief like when I would take off that heavy rucksack that I carried during my short time in the military. I felt a feeling I had never felt in my life. A peace came over me like I have never experienced before. I was finally free!

Beloved, never avenge yourselves, but leave the way open for God's wrath [and His judicial righteousness]; for it is written [in Scripture], "VENGEANCE IS MINE, I WILL REPAY," says the Lord. Romans 12:19

Steps for Moving Forward

....

1. Acknowledge your contribution in the matter. Do not waste time pointing the finger at everyone else without taking a hard look at you.
2. Be careful how you seek counsel during challenging times. Sometimes, having itching ears will help contribute to the problem when you are truly seeking help.
3. Ask God to connect you with individuals who have your best interest at heart and who will point you in the right direction.
4. Stay connected to the Word of God so that you are equipped with the tools and strategies you need to overcome challenging situations.

Chapter 3

How to Forgive Yourself

What about you? Yes you. Over time, you will learn that forgiveness is always more about you than the other person. You must start with you first because most of the time, you are staring the problem right in the face every time you look in the mirror. Yes, if we are honest with ourselves, sometimes it is us. I know that is probably not what you want to hear, but it is the truth. Remember, the Bible says that we must forgive seventy-seven times seven. Yeah, I know. No matter how you look at it, that is a huge pill to swallow. In earlier years, I thought people had to earn my forgiveness by doing what I wanted and saying what I wanted when I wanted them to say it with no delays. What I later realized was that we cannot expect God to forgive us if we cannot fully love and forgive His children, no matter who they are and no matter what they have done. Whew! I know that is a big task for sure. You mean I need to forgive even the most hideous of offenses and the biggest pile of false accusations and lies? Yes, even all of that! You see, the greatest commandment of all is to **love**. Love will keep you from committing a multitude of crimes against others that some of them probably deserve if you are measuring it from your measuring stick. Yes, you will have to forgive and love those who you really wanted to beat up if you want to be free. We must be fully aware that if we pray to God and we have not forgiven our brother or sister, we do not really know Him. That is what the Word of God says. I had read that scripture multiple times, but this time, it was as if the scales were removed from my eyes because I experienced clarity like never before. If you have not done this already, start with you first. Forgive yourself for every time you allowed yourself to get entangled with emotions because "they" hurt you or said something you did not like. Forgive yourself for every time you leaned on your own understanding instead of God. Forgive yourself for every time you took the bait and fired back instead of walking away. Forgive yourself for using your words as weapons of mass destruction, destroying all who ever hurt you and got in your path. Forgive yourself for beating yourself up about something that was beyond your control.

You may be wondering if you really have to forgive yourself. The answer is a resounding YES! The enemy wants you to remain in bondage. He wants you to beat yourself up, and ultimately desires for you to self-destruct and remain in isolation because of your past. Let me remind you that you are not what happened to you, and you are not your past. Satan will try to infiltrate your mind and plant seeds of lies, toxic emotions, self-demeaning thoughts, and assumptions to get you off course. Guess what? Ain't nobody got time for that. Yes, I said "ain't" and I meant it lol. The Bible tells us in John 8:44 that satan is the father of lies. He is the original liar and the godfather of lies. He is the one who told the very first lie in all creation. He distracted Eve in the garden of Eden and caused her to sin against God based on a nasty, deceitful, lie that he made look undeniably appetizing at that moment. It is his duty to distract us so that we will be more entangled in his nasty little web of lies, considering everything that is contrary to the Word of God instead of standing on exactly what the Word of God says and fulfilling our God-given purpose in life.

> *He was a murderer from the beginning, and abode not in the truth, because there is no truth in him. When he speaketh a lie, he*

Forgiveness is the Key to Freedom

speaketh of his own: for he is a liar, and the father of it. John 8:44 KJV

No matter what your past looks like, no matter what you have done, no matter what you have endured in life, I assure you that God is waiting for you with open arms. He loves you unconditionally regardless of how reckless, selfish, and ugly your past is and regardless of how badly you may feel about the events that have occurred. God will take what you view as a mess and turn it into a message to help others. When you fully surrender yourselves to His will and His way, repent of your sins, turn from your wicked ways, and truly accept Him as your Lord and Savior, He will move those mountainous situations out of your lives. Those mountains will no longer hold you hostage or keep you bound. No. Freedom is your portion, joy is your portion, and peace is your portion. God loves you and most importantly, He has forgiven you as if you have never sinned. He does not have all your sins tied to a string ready to dangle them over your head every time you make a mistake, so you must forgive yourself. Ask the Holy Spirit to lead and guide you through this process and He will see you through. I am not saying that it will be easy, but it is necessary, and the rewards are truly beneficial in the end. In 1 Samuel 15:22, Samuel was trying to get Saul to understand that obedience is always better than sacrifice. This means that it is better for us that we obey the Word of God above all and above what you think you should do because sometimes we follow our own ways and our ways often get us in trouble. Saul thought he was getting away with his lie, but God knows and sees all. We can run, but we cannot hide from God.

> *Samuel said, "Has the LORD as great a delight in burnt offerings and sacrifices as in obedience to the voice of the LORD? Behold, to obey is better than sacrifice, And to heed [is better] than the fat of rams. 1 Samuel 15:22 AMP*

The best thing you can do when faced with adversity is cast your cares on God. Ask the Holy Spirit to help you. Talk to Him about what you are facing. He will never lead you astray. He will lead you and guide you every step of the way. Do not think for one second that you are damaged goods because of the path you have walked in life. Repent, ask God for forgiveness, turn away from that old life, and embrace the new you. Give God an opportunity to clean you up from the pain and misery of your past and give you peace that surpasses all understanding. I'm talking about the kind of peace that has those around you wondering why you are so happy when in their eyes you should be crumbling to pieces. The fact that you still have life and breath in your body is evidence that God has His hand on your life.

Use your testimony to help pull someone else out the very pit you once found yourself in. Do not be afraid to share how gracious God has been to you. He will use what seems like trash to others and present it like a rare precious jewel on a platter. You may have allowed the enemy to infiltrate your mind and cause you to believe that you are busted, disgusted, and useless, and that God cannot use someone like you. Can I remind you that before you were formed in the womb of your mother that God had great plans for you? He knew the mistakes that you would make and he loves you anyway.

> *Before I formed thee in the belly I knew thee; and before thou camest forth out of the womb I sanctified thee. Jeremiah 1:5KJV*

Proclaim your freedom today. Shout to the mountaintops that you are you free! Thank God for forgiving you and using you for His glory. Do not let anyone cause you to believe that you deserve less than God's best for you because of your past. They think they know, but they have no idea the plans God has in store for you, so from today forward, walk with your head held high. Be confident knowing who you are and whose you are – a child of the Most High God who loves you unconditionally, flaws and all.

How to Forgive Yourself

....

1. Start with repentance. Ask God to forgive you of your sins and the things you have done that were not pleasing in His sight.
2. Write a letter to yourself. Start with I forgive myself for_____.
3. Thank God for forgiving you and setting you free.
4. Strive to follow God's example every day.
5. Love yourself!

Chapter 4

Forgiveness Will Set You Free!

Have you buried problems, situations, and people at the back of your mind, hoping that you will never have to deal with them if you keep them buried? One of the biggest mistakes we make is avoiding problems, people, and situations instead of dealing with the problems that got you to the point of despair. Ignoring problems in hopes that they will eventually go away on their own is a sure recipe for disaster. At some point, you must deal with the pain of your past. No matter what has taken place, God's wonderful grace is more abundant than any sin committed, as stated in Romans 5:20. You have work to do. Don't waste any more time missing out on all God has for you because of your past.

Forgiveness is the Key to Freedom

God's law was given so that all people could see how sinful they were. But as people sinned more and more, God's wonderful grace became more abundant. Romans 5:20 NLT

An unforgiving heart is like a burden, a weight, or a load. It's too heavy to carry. That big "F" word – forgiveness – that causes some to cringe and that some view as very expensive and most definitely an earned treasure, will set you free. Let's look at the meaning of the word "forgive." Forgive means to no longer feel angry about or wish to punish (an offence, flaw, or mistake), to stop feeling angry or resentful towards (someone) for an offence, flaw, or mistake. It also means to cancel a debt. So what God is commanding you to do is to wipe the slate clean and cancel all debts of those who have offended you. You can cancel all debts and love those who have offended you from a place that does not require you to be in direct contact with those who have offended you, especially if it is a situation where physical, sexual, or mental abuse has taken place.

Please keep in mind that unforgiveness is very dangerous. It is like being in a hostage situation because what you are doing is holding someone in your heart and mind like a seed planted in the ground, but instead of reaping a harvest of beauty, joy, and peace, you reap a harvest of bitterness and strife and every negative thing you can imagine. Often, unforgiveness, which is rooted and grounded in the spirit of offense, becomes a snare in our lives if left unchecked.

> *"Then said He unto to His disciples, "It is impossible but that offences will come: but woe unto him, through whom they come. ² It were better for him that a millstone were hanged about his neck, and he cast into the sea, than that he should offend one of these little ones. ³ Take heed to yourselves: If thy brother trespass against thee, rebuke him; and if he repents, forgive him. ⁴ And if he trespass against thee seven times in a day, and seven times in a day turn again to thee, saying, I repent; thou shalt forgive Him." Luke 17:1-4*

Let's look at Joseph. His brothers became jealous and as a result, they concocted a plan to get rid of him. They were so determined to carry out their evil act that they even thought about killing him and lying to their father about his location. Here, we discover that God had another plan for his life. He used the older brother Reuben to divert the plan and instead of killing him, they put him into a pit. Some Midianite traders passed by after Joseph was placed in that pit beyond his will, as recorded in Genesis 37:28, and sold Joseph to the Ishmeelites for twenty pieces of silver. The beauty here, to make a long story short, is that even though Joseph's brothers had committed such a horrendous act against him, he still chose to not only forgive them, but he blessed them in their time of need. What a great example to follow.

What we can learn from Joseph is that there will always be plenty of opportunities to become offended, but the true test is how you handle offense when it comes knocking on your door looking to cause trouble, inflict pain, and initiate chaos in your life. Will you allow offense into your heart? Will you take the bait? You must ask yourselves these questions when troubles arise. You must frisk every idea down at the door of your hearts before it has an opportunity to take root in your heart. Sometimes, those you love, cherish, and hold dear to your heart are the very people who will offend you and vice versa. Those closest to you who you would least expect will sometimes have you questioning God. If we are brutally honest with ourselves, we will admit that sometimes the problem is us and we sometimes cause hurt and pain in the lives of others. It goes right back to the saying "hurt people, hurt people." In my situation, I found myself on both sides at different times in my life because I allowed myself to be offended by the actions and words of others and I therefore wreaked havoc with my actions and with my words. I used my words as weapons, lashing back with the intent to hurt them like they hurt me. It was a never-ending, vicious cycle and pattern of toxicity and destruction. If you continue down this path, you will always find yourselves in a hostage type of situation. Here is some good news. God is the greatest negotiator in every hostage situation you may find yourselves in, and I could not have said it better than Moses when he petitioned Pharaoh to let his people go.

I will be honest with you and tell you that it will not always be easy, but it will always be worth it. Everything that is good for you may not always taste good. I must inform you that it may not be as sweet as sugar or taste like honey in a honeycomb, but at the end of the day, a decision must be made, and you will be happy you did. Ask yourself some more questions at this point. Are you going to let unforgiveness hinder you from doing what God has called you to do because you are holding people in your heart and mind? Are you going to continue to give satan the keys to your heart and let him terrorize you to no end? If I can offer some advice, I will tell you it is not worth it. Forgive, let it go, and be at peace. Release them, yes, every one of them, and be free! This reminds me of David because unforgiveness is like a huge giant in your life, but just as David faced Goliath with no fear, you too can face that giant in your life today. Pick up your stones like David did. Yes, pick up those stones of peace, joy, love, and happiness, and tear that Goliath in your life down to shreds. You can do it. Everyone thought David was crazy because they sized him up to his giant that was obviously much bigger in stature, but I am here to tell you that there is no mountain too big and no situation too challenging for God to intervene. Nothing is impossible for Him. He is a God who can take impossible situations and circumstances and turn them completely around for your good. Initially it does sound a bit too good to be true, but guess what? That is the truth. The Word tells us this in Luke 1:37, that nothing is impossible with God.

For with God nothing shall be impossible. Luke 1:37

He will take those situations you thought were beyond repair and do what you thought was impossible. Just because it appears hard to you does not mean that it is too hard for God. Forgiveness is not an option. It is essential. I will be completely honest with you and tell you that forgiveness is hard when we try to do it on our own, but when you take that burden off your back and place it into the hands of your loving Father, He will handle the situation better than you ever thought you could. You cannot avoid this part of the journey. Turn it over to Him. It is vital to your walk with Christ, and in the end, it is you that really wins. Allow God to do a new work in you. Let Him mold you, shape you, transform you, and deliver you from the bondage that you are in, and show you how to forgive yourself and others.

God has a way of using that ugly, embarrassing, taunting, situation in your life as a way for you to help pull your brother or sister out of a dark place. You see, the Bible says that they overcame by the blood of the lamb and by the word of their testimony. I am not telling you about something I have no knowledge or experience in. I had to walk this path myself holding His hand every step of the way. I had to turn the other cheek when I was rejected, falsely accused, and mistreated. I had to forgive and "L. I. G." (LET IT GO). The mere thought of how God sent His only son to die on an old, rugged cross for our sins way back on Calvary convicted me. Jesus paid the price for us all. He stood in our place. He was persecuted, beaten, and falsely accused. He paid the price for sins He never committed. Who am I to hold someone in my heart and mind who God loves? What was I thinking? Your next questions might be how exactly do I forgive? How do I really benefit from forgiveness? Unforgiveness gives satan full access and permission to wreak havoc in your life until you make the decision to be delivered from his web of entanglement and be set free. I would encourage you to get in a place and posture of forgiveness so much so that you are the least bit offended when someone says or does something that offends you. I pray that your go to for offense will always be forgiveness. Forgive as quickly as you are offended. It will surely do your heart good. You will find yourself looking, feeling, eating, and sleeping better because all that anger and bitterness can cause you to lose your peace, joy, and happiness, and even affect your health. Satan tries to set traps for us and make us think that we are justified in our offense and before you know it, you have replayed the thoughts in your mind several times over like a broken record. You may even meditate on the acts of injustice and after a short time, that is all you talk about, unconsciously aware that the enemy has caught you once again and entangled you in his web of lies and deceit. Tell yourself repeatedly that unforgiveness is not worth your peace and salvation. Most importantly, it is not in alignment with what God's Word says. Why did I say forgive as quickly as you are offended? Because offenses are inevitable. The Bible says that offense will come, but the question is how will you handle it? Will you save a seat for satan in your life and let him drive you down misery lane all because someone offended you, or said something that you didn't like, or did something to you that you felt like you did not deserve? Or will you choose to rise above it all and take the high road, fly high like an eagle, and soar without a care in this world knowing that your Father in heaven has you covered? Think about it, and while you are pondering on that, let me remind you *that **forgiveness is the key to freedom.***

Command satan to take his hand off your heart and off your mind and to let you go in the name of Jesus! Repeat after me. Say "I am free!" Say it with boldness, with undeniable confidence, and without any doubt because you are free! Walk in freedom from today forward because He has truly set you free. The Word tells us in John Chapter 8 that whoever the Son sets free is free indeed! Take a moment right now, pause whatever you are doing, and thank God for setting you free! You are free from the hurt, shame, rejection, fear, etc. You are free at last. Thank God that you are free indeed. My prayer is that you will continue to walk in this newfound freedom and that you will love others as Christ has loved you. And that you will love your neighbor as you love yourself even when you do not want to do it or when it is a challenge. Be intentional about seeing others through the lens of love. The lens of love filters out all the negativity and gives you the ability to love others even if you must love them from afar. You can only withhold forgiveness for others if there is no love in your heart. Ask God to search your heart today, remove every stony place from your heart, and give you a heart of flesh, a heart that loves and forgives.

> *"And above all things have fervent love for one another, for "love will cover a multitude of sins." 1 Peter 4:8*

Steps to Becoming Free

....

1. Release those who have offended you from that place of unforgiveness.
2. Do not allow offense to take a seat in your heart and mind.
3. Let it go. Lock the door and throw away the key.
4. Be very aware of satan's plots and schemes. Do not allow him to get you entangled in your past.
5. Repent of your sins, turn from your wicked ways, and ask God for forgiveness.

Chapter 5

Learn to Identify God's Hand in the Midst of Chaos

By now you may be asking, "Where is God in all of this?" or "Does He see what I am going through?" or "But why me?" Let me assure you that Abba Father wants the absolute best for all His children, even you. It is not His desire that we live in misery, despair, and gloom. We sometimes find ourselves going down these paths as a direct result of the choices we make. To find out which decisions we should be making, we must seek God and spend time in His presence, reading His word and in prayer communicating with Him while pausing long enough to hear what He has to say. Have you ever heard someone say, "The very answer to your problem is found in His presence?" I have had plenty of people ask me how this was even possible because they felt like God has never spoken to them or heard their cry. The more time we spend praying and reading the Word and taking some extra time just to sit in His presence and listen with an open heart and mind, His voice will become so relevant and prevalent in your life. You will begin to decipher when and how He speaks to you, when He is not speaking, and when the enemy is speaking and attempting to infiltrate your heart and mind. God will speak to you in various ways. Sometimes, He may speak a Word to you through a song you listen to, through the scripture you read, or through someone or something. He speaks to us in various ways, but we are often too busy to notice because we are so fixated and caught up with ourselves and others. Did you know that when you are facing those valley situations where you feel all alone that God is right there with you?

> *Be strong and of good courage, do not fear nor be afraid of them; for the Lord your God, He is the one who goes with you. He will not leave you or forsake you. Deuteronomy 31:6*

I know you may be feeling abandoned and alone sometimes. You may even feel like God does not hear your earnest plea and cry for help. I assure you; He is always with you through the good, bad, and ugly. He was right there when you gave that friend, family member, in-law, or neighbor "the business," yet He still loves, blesses, and provides for us anyway. Now that is what you call a friend, and we certainly have a friend in Jesus. There is absolutely no one who can love us quite like He does, but there are those that come very close.

I pray that God will continue to speak to your heart, your mind, and your soul. May He give you a new outlook on life and an understanding of the importance of forgiveness. Be more cognizant of what people do and say that comes off as offensive to you and take notes in your journal about your progress and strides in the right direction. You may have to press the reset button several times, but it will be worth it in the long run. You may even find yourself looking back over certain situations and scenarios and wonder why you handled them the way you did in the past and be able to compare it to your current progress as a testament to your growth in this area. Remember, forgiveness is for you. It is good for your soul and is required of everyone who calls themselves a child of God. Never put yourself in a predicament where you are contemplating whether you should forgive someone. At the first sight of offense, let your first defense always be forgiveness rather than bitterness, resentment, and unforgiveness. When doubt starts to creep in and feelings of despair seem to linger, rest assured that you can do all things through Christ who gives you strength. Yes, even the hard things. He will see you through it all, but you must stay the course and continue walking the path to freedom. You will be so happy you did. Family members, friends, co-workers etc. may have hurt you along the way with their words and actions, but remember, God is on your side, favor is on your side, and your victory is on the other side of this mountain. Mountain? Yes, the Word tells us in Mark 11:23 (NLT): "I tell you the truth, you can say to this mountain, may you be lifted up and thrown into the sea, and it will happen." You must really believe it will happen for you and have no doubt in your heart about it. I encourage you to stop talking about those mountains in your life and command them to get out of your way and watch how things start to shift in your life for the better.

How to Identify God's Hand

....

1. Be intentional about spending time with God every day.
2. Stay connected to His Word.
3. Keep a journal of your progress to identify ways that God has been leading and guiding you through challenging situations.
4. Speak life!

Chapter 6

Forgiveness Does Not Always Equate to Reconnection

I admonish you not to get stuck thinking that because you forgive someone that it means that they are automatically granted full access back into your life. Some shy away from forgiveness altogether because they believe that if they forgive someone, it automatically gives those who have hurt them an invitation and a ticket to a first-class seat back into their life. Can I let you in on a little secret? Forgiveness does not mean that you must be buddies, pals, or friends again. Forgiveness means that you have chosen to walk down the path of freedom and that you have decided to love others as the Lord so graciously loves you and that you have decided to forgive others as He has so graciously forgiven us time and time again. Most importantly, forgiveness means that you have decided to walk in obedience to God. Forgiveness has never been about tallying up all the wrongs committed against you. It is more about being willing to throw the scoreboard away with the willingness to love others who have hurt you. This same principle should be applied to you and those you may have hurt as well. Yes, some relationships warrant restoration without a shadow of doubt, while others most definitely need to be dissolved. This can be challenging because you may have to love some family members from afar, especially when they are continuing down the path of toxicity and trying to wreak havoc in your life with their words and actions pulling you into an unending cycle of pain and turmoil. That does not mean that you do not love them. It simply means that you love yourself enough that you will not allow satan to take you down misery lane again at the expense of your peace. It is God's desire that we all live in harmony, loving one another. It was never included anywhere in His plan to have us living in despair because of broken relationships, but everyone does not reach this realization or revelation at the same time. You may have experienced brokenness in your life that catapulted you into this terrible cycle of unforgiveness that caused you to say and do some things that are not reflective of a child of God, and you are not sure if you can and should reconnect with someone. This is when you pause, ask the Holy

Spirit for guidance on how to move forward, and follow His lead every step of the way.

This process can be quite challenging for some, but I assure you that if you follow God's lead, He will not lead you astray. Do not allow your emotions to overshadow the steps you must take. God will give you clear signs and instructions on how to proceed, whether you like the instructions or not. I pray that God gives you the wisdom to discern which path you must take because the decision you make here is crucial to your walk to freedom. No matter how hard it seems, reach out to Lord and ask the Holy Spirit to lead you and guide you down this pathway to freedom. It is most definitely a journey – one that can that change the very fabric and footprint of your life for the better. I assure you that before you know it, you will be wondering how you made it to the other side of opposition, and how that humongous mountain was removed from your path, or how that sycamine tree was plucked up and cast into the sea. Remember, it is God's desire that you be healed, delivered, and set free. He always has a plan to prosper you no matter what you face on this journey called life. He wants the absolute best for you because He loves you that much.

I can honestly say that I was very disappointed in the people in my life for what took place, but I am so happy that today I can confidently say without a shadow of any doubt that I LOVE them and wish God's absolute best for them. I pray that I have encouraged you to do the same. Yes, they may have hurt you to your core, but forgive anyway, love them anyway, bless them anyway, and watch how God blesses you for your obedience. Forgive and walk in freedom. Remember, ***forgiveness is the key to freedom*** and it will change the whole trajectory of your life!

How to Identify if a Relationship Calls for Reconciliation or Disconnection

1. You and the other individual have had an open conversation about what has taken place and have extended forgiveness to each other.
2. You have peace in your heart about moving forward after praying and seeking God about the situation.
3. All parties agree to respect each other's boundaries.
4. Has the behavior of the individual changed or are they still trying to keep you in perpetual cycles even after laying everything out on the table?

Prayers for Forgiveness

1. Lord, thank You for opening my eyes and turning me from darkness to light and from the power of satan in the mighty name of Jesus. Acts 26:18
2. Lord, thank You for redeeming me through the blood of Jesus and forgiving me of my sins in the mighty name of Jesus. Colossians 1:14
3. Lord, I confess all my sins (pause and confess any sins you may have committed knowingly and unknowingly) and I believe that You are faithful and will forgive me and purify me. I John 1:9
4. Lord, I forgive everyone who has hurt me by their words and actions. I believe that You will forgive me as I continue to forgive those who offend me in the mighty name of Jesus. Matthew 6:14
5. Lord, please help me to be kind to others even though they plot evil against me in the mighty name of Jesus. Ephesians 4:32

6. Lord, have mercy on me and blot out all my transgressions in the mighty name of Jesus. Psalm 51:1-2
7. Lord, I release everyone that I have been holding in my heart and mind because of what they said or did to me. Matthew 6:14-15
8. Lord, thank You for giving me the grace to forgive a multitude of sins. Matthew 18:21-22
9. Lord, please forgive me for every time I have used my mouth as a weapon of mass destruction against myself and others. Proverbs 18:21
10. Lord, thank You for forgiving me of all my sins and transgressions.
11. Lord, I choose to walk in obedience to Your Word from this day forward.
12. Lord thank You for Your grace and mercy even when I do not deserve it. Lamentations 3:22-23
13. Lord, thank You for forgiving me and loving me as if I have never sinned. Jeremiah 31:34
14. Lord, thank You for giving me a tender heart towards those who have hurt me. Ephesians 4:32

15. Lord, I release myself from all the hurt, bitterness, rejection, and negative emotions connected to individuals in my life. I choose to walk in obedience and freedom, forgiving others as quicky as offense comes. I forgive myself and release myself into total freedom.

All these prayers I release to You Lord and pray in the mighty name of Jesus, Amen!

Closure

By now, we have learned some very useful tips, strategies, dos, and don'ts as it relates to forgiveness. Whew, what a journey it has been. After you have taken some time to pause and reflect, ask yourself some questions. Are there people in your life that you need to forgive? Do you need to ask those you have hurt for forgiveness? I encourage you to forgive them and let it go. Your life and salvation are dependent on this very important step. If that person you need to forgive is no longer living, write a note of forgiveness, sign your name to it, then pray and ask God to release you from the pain caused by that person and pain you may have caused them and rip it to shreds. You are forgiven! How can I be so sure? Well, the Word says in John 8:36, "So if the Son sets you free you are free indeed." You are free! Declare it! Decree it! It is so in the mighty name of Jesus! From today, forward walk with your head held high and be confident knowing that you are free. You are free from the pain of your past and free from the pain of living in toxic cycles of unforgiveness. Take some time and thank God for the work He has done in your life because He is so worthy of your praise. He did not have to rescue you, He did not have to save you, but He did. He is a real good Father and there is no other Father in this world quite like Him.

Can I tell you something? *Forgiveness is the key to freedom.* Do not allow yourself to get to a place where you are ashamed to tell your testimony. Someone is waiting for hope that they too can overcome unfortunate situations. There is someone out there who has been hurt to their core and they feel like there is no way out. Your story can help pull them out of that dark pit of despair. Your story matters in more ways than you know. Remember, God is not looking for people who think they have it all together who love to portray a certain image to others. That is far from authentic. He is looking for people who are willing to acknowledge their sin and admit that they need help and God's grace daily.

> Forgive and walk in freedom
> from this day forward. Freedom
> looks so good on you!

~ Selah

30 Keys to Freedom

Here are some keys to help you walk through the journey of forgiveness daily. Sometimes you must forgive in faith because forgiveness does not erase the hurt and pain. When you decide to forgive it means that you have decided to walk in obedience to God no matter how painful it may seem. It may be a challenging task to complete on your own and many just do not know what forgiveness looks like or understand how it is possible after just heartache and pain. It may be hard in your eyes but remember, nothing is impossible with God. Ask the Holy Spirit to lead and guide you every step of the way.

Use these keys as a daily guide to keep you on the right track. Track your progress and write notes to yourself and God daily. If you veer off on the wrong path it is okay, regroup and start again. Remember, *Forgiveness is the Key to Freedom.*

Key 1

In whom we have redemption through His blood, even the forgiveness of sins. Colossians 1:14

I decree and declare that I have redemption and forgiveness through the Blood of Jesus.

Key 2

Blessed is he whose transgression is forgiven, whose sin is covered. Psalm 32:1

I decree and declare that my sins are forgiven.

Key 3

But He being full of compassion, forgave their iniquity and destroyed them not, yea many a time turned He, His anger away and did not stir up His wrath.
Psalm 78:38

I decree and declare that God
had compassion on me.

Key 4

Who forgiveth all thine iniquities; who health all our diseases. Psalm 103:3

I decree and declare that God has healed every disease that was dwelling within me.

Key 5

And they shall teach no more every man his neighbor, and every man his brother saying know the Lord: for they shall all know me, from the least of them to the greatest of them, saith the Lord: for I will forgive their iniquity and I will remember their sin no more.
Jeremiah 31:34

I decree and declare that God has forgiven me as if I have never sinned.

Key 6

And forgive us our debts as we forgive our debtors.
Matthew 6:12

I decree and declare that I have forgiven
my debtors and God has forgiven me.

Key 7

For if ye forgive men their trespasses, your heavenly Father will also for give you. But if ye forgive not men their trespasses neither will your Father forgive your trespasses. Matthew 6:14-15

I decree and declare that I am forgiven because I have decided to walk in obedience to God.

Key 8

But that ye may know that the Son of man hath power on earth to forgive sins, (then said He to the sick of palsy) Arise and walk? But that ye may know that the Son of man hath power on earth to forgive sins. Arise take up your bed and go unto thine house.
Matthew 9:6-7

I decree and declare that I have confidence knowing that God has the power to forgive sins.

Key 9

Then came Peter to Him and said, Lord, how often shall my brother sin against me, and I forgive him? Till seven times? Jesus saith unto him, I say not unto thee until seven times but until seventy times seven.
Matthew 18:21-22

I decree and declare that God has
given me the grace to forgive.

Key 10

Judge not and ye shall not be judged: condemn not, and ye shall be condemned: forgive, and ye shall be forgiven. Luke 6:37

I decree and declare that I am
obedient to the Word of God.

Key 11

Take heed to yourselves: If thy brother trespass against thee rebuke him, and if he repent forgive him. And if he trespass against thee seven times in a day turn again to thee, saying I repent, thou shalt forgive him. Luke 17:3-4

I decree and declare that I will
forgive those who hurt me.

Key 12

And be ye kind to one another, tender hearted forgiving one another, even as God for Christ's sake hath forgiven you. Ephesians 4:32

I decree and declare that I have a tender heart towards others.

FORGIVENESS IS THE KEY TO FREEDOM

Key 13

Forbearing one another and forgiving one another, if any man have a quarrel against any even as Christ forgave you so also do ye. Colossians 3:13

I decree and declare that I will forgive others no matter what.

Key 14

Rejoice not when thine enemy falleth, and let not thine heart be glad when he stumbleth: Lest the Lord see it, and it displease him, and he turn away his wrath from him. Proverbs 24:17-18

I decree and declare that I pray for my
enemies when they stumble.

Key 15

Be not overcome of evil, but overcome evil with good. Romans 12:21

I decree and declare that I will not repay evil for evil.

Key 16

But I sat unto you, love your enemies, bless them that curse you, do good to them that hate you, and pray for them which despitefully use you, and persecute you: That ye may be the children of your Father which is in heaven: for He maketh His sun to rise on the evil and on the good, and sendeth rain on the just and on the unjust. For if ye love them which love you, what reward have ye? Do not even the publicans the same? Matthew 5:44-46

I decree and declare that I love my enemies.

Key 17

To speak evil of no man, to be no brawlers, but gentle, shewing all meekness unto all men. Titus 3:2

I decree and declare that I am gentle
and meek towards all men.

Key 18

Seeing it is a righteous thing with God to recompense tribulation to them that trouble you. 2 Thessalonians 1:6

I decree and declare that I will let God
take care of those that trouble me.

Key 19

Dearly beloved, avenge not yourselves, but rather give place unto wrath: for it is written, vengeance is I will repay, saith the Lord. Romans 12:19

I decree and declare that vengeance belongs to God not me.

Key 20

To me belongeth vengeance, and recompense; their foot shall slide in due time: for the day of their calamity is at hand, and the things that shall come upon them make haste. Deuteronomy 32:35

I declare and decree that I will
let God fight my battles.

Key 21

Therefore if thine enemy hunger, feed him; if he thirst, give him drink: for in so doing thou shalt heap coals of fire on his head. Romans 12:20

I decree and declare that I am gentle
and meek towards all men.

Key 22

If thine enemy be hungry, give him bread to eat and if he be thirsty, give him water to drink: Proverbs 25:21

I decree and declare that I will bless
those who wish evil towards me.

Forgiveness is the Key to Freedom

Key 23

And when ye stand praying, forgive, if ye have ought against any: that your Father also which is in heaven may forgive you your trespasses. But if ye do not forgive, neither will your Father which is in heaven forgive your trespasses. Mark 11:25-26

I decree and declare that I will not walk
in disobedience to God's Word.

Key 24

If a man say, I love God, and he hateth his brother, he is a liar: for he that loveth not his brother whom he hath seen, how can he love God whom he hath not seen? 1 John 4:20

I decree and declare that I love others because God has commanded me to.

Key 25

Whosoever hateth his brother is a murderer: and ye know that no murderer hath eternal life abiding in Him. 1 John 3:15

I decree and declare that hate has
no place in my heart.

Key 26

When a man's ways please the Lord, He maketh even his enemies to be at peace with him. Proverbs 16:7

I decree and declare that my ways are
pleasing and acceptable to God.

Key 27

Not rendering evil for evil or railing for railing: but contrariwise blessing; knowing that ye are thereunto called, that ye should inherit a blessing. 1 Peter 3:9

I decree and declare that I will bless
those who wish evil towards me.

Key 28

But if thou shalt indeed obey His voice, and do all that I speak; then will I be an enemy unto thine enemies, and an adversary unto thine adversaries. Exodus 23:22

I decree and declare that I obey the voice of God.

Key 29

But love your enemies, and do good, and lend, hoping for nothing again: and your reward shall be great, and ye shall be the children of the Highest: for He is kind to the unthankful and to the evil. Luke 6:35

I decree and declare that I do good to
all expecting nothing in return.

Key 30

But thou hast saved us from our enemies, and hast put them to shame that hated us. Psalm 44:7

I decree and declare that God will
save me from my enemies.

Congratulations! You made it through the month with your keys to freedom. I pray that these scriptures (keys) will help set your life in order and be foundational in all that you do. Continue to read God's Word daily, spend time in His presence, and seek Him like your life is dependent on it because it is. Speak life no matter what and always remember that *Forgiveness is the Key to Freedom*. Refuse to partner with satan another day to use your words as weapons of mass destruction against yourself and others. Be free!

Made in the USA
Columbia, SC
05 September 2023